KATA AND KUMITE
FOR KARATE

Chris Thompson

Edited by Paul Crompton

Paul H. Crompton Ltd.
94 Felsham Road
London SW15 1DQ
England

First Edition 1997
© 1993 Chris Thompson
ISBN No 1-874250-55-3

London: Paul H. Crompton Ltd.
94 Felsham Road, London SW15 1DQ, England

New York: Talman Company
131 Spring Street, New York, N.Y. 10012, U.S.A.

Printed and bound in England
by Caric Print Ltd.
Clerwood, Corunna Main,
Andover, Hants SP10 1JE
(01264) 354887

CONTENTS

Preface..5

Introduction 6

Renraku-waza...7

Attacks 31

Counter-Attacks 45

Kata 60

Bassai..62

Wanshu 75

Ji'in 86

Rohai 99

Useishi 107

Kata Notes...120

Ji-Yu Kumite..122

Summary 123

A SPECIAL THANK YOU TO:

Steve Heybourne - For his patience whilst taking all the photographs

Darren Pattenden - For his painting of the front cover

Neville Smith - For his assistance with all the pair techniques

Alison Thompson - For her invaluable assistance in creating this book

Preface

The Okinawan Karate Masters of the 19th Century did not want the secrets of Karate to leave their small island. This martial Art had been developed and refined over many years in total secrecy, usually in the dead of night, and kept within the family circle.

When Karate was inevitably introduced to mainland Japan in the early 20th Century, the Masters still had serious reservations. Their concern was that by teaching Karate to the masses the true essence of Karate would be lost. Physical technique would be taught with a total disregard of the mental training and in the wrong hands the art of Karate would be totally misused.

In order to prevent all the true secrets and knowledge of Karate being passed on it is believed the early Okinawan Masters who taught on the Japanese mainland held back the true explanation of technique. It is unclear as to the extent of technique withheld, but for many years as Karate was exported throughout the world, it was an incomplete system being taught.

In the 30 years since I began studying Karate, there have been significant changes for the better in the art. Two major changes have been in the way Karate is taught and in the in-depth explanation of Karate application. It is in this area where curiosity has led to greater research into Karate's history, to unlock the true origins of the application of technique.

It is Kata that holds many of the secrets of these old Okinawan Masters. Many techniques that make up Kata are either totally disguised or have been misinterpreted. Many senior karate-ka of all nationalities have questioned what they have learnt and through methodical and diligent research in Japan, Okinawa and China, are beginning to unravel this gigantic puzzle.

It is an exciting time for karate-ka in Karate's evolution, whether they be long-standing participants or newly-joined students of this fascinating Martial Art. Even as Karate enters this new phase, its popularity is greater than ever and at last the true benefits of this discipline are being recognised.

The shroud of mystery is slowly lifting, but there are still many unanswered questions.

Introduction

The three areas of karate I have covered in detail for this book are combination techniques (Renraku Waza), pair techniques (Yakusoku Kumite) and Kata (formal exercises).

I have shown many combinations using as many varied techniques as possible. These range from quite simple moves to techniques with a degree of difficulty.

In the pairs section, there are over 20 examples of offensive and defensive techniques.

Finally, I have shown five Kata which are all personal favourites as well as being quite advanced.

All three subjects covered are important in a sound training programme and emphasis must be placed on them equally in order to maintain a high standard of karate.

I have found throughout all the clubs in my Association that by training and polishing technique in these three areas a well-rounded and competent Karate-ka is produced.

I hope this book will be a valuable training aid for the serious karate-ka, irrespective of style.

Chris Thompson

CHAPTER I

Renraku Waza

A relentless onslaught of attacking techniques best describes Renraku-Waza. These techniques in my opinion still come under Kihon. Many senior instructors have separated them from basics and given them their own identity. I can understand some of the reasons for this, but it depends on how they teach karate and where the emphasis is placed in that particular school of karate. I teach a traditional style of karate with emphasis on the kihon, kata and kumite. Renraku-Waza is simply putting kihon techniques together. Therefore by putting strong, simple, basic techniques into a combination of strong basic movements, you create a more efficient attack with a greater chance of defeating your opponent. This is also true of defence and counter-attacks.

Most of you are taught in your club, regardless of which style you practice, to try and stop and drop your opponent with one technique. This is still the ideal training goal as it focuses the mind and aims to increase the 'kime' in each technique delivered whilst training. I am sure you have had the satisfaction of stopping your opponent in his tracks with a single technique, good balance and lots of speed. Also your opponent may have made a mistake and you obviously made him pay dearly for it.

Unfortunately, this scenario does not happen very frequently with Ippon Waza (single technique), but by using Renraku-Waza you can create the circumstances to drop your opponent.

When practising Renraku-Waza in the dojo, whether on your own, or in the line, you must always visualise your opponents. Always train to keep full control of your body, placing your foot and hand techniques accurately at the imaginary target.

- Speed is essential, along with good posture, balance and breathing.
- Always complete your combination with a strong kiai.

Sometimes practice delivering all your techniques to one level, for example all at Chudan level (middle section). Then again, practice delivering techniques at various heights, such as a Jodan (head) punch, followed by a Chudan kick, then a groin strike.

This type of practice will give you flexibility as well as stamina and strength.

When Renraku-Waza is used in actual free fighting (Jissen), then your hard training will pay dividends. It is the ability to attack with combinations, yet vary your striking targets in a split second, that will make you the superior fighter.

Obviously, your opponent will dictate where your attacks are thrown, by his positioning, either prior to or during an exchange of techniques.

Why is it so important to continuously practice Renraku-Waza? When you face a karate-ka in Ji-Yu Kumite or Shiai (competition) and there is no opening, then you have to create one. There are many ways to do this, one example is Ashi Barai (foot sweep), and your Sensei will show you many more. Once the opening is there, then Renraku-Waza plays a vital role, as it is knowing how and where to follow up that counts. How many times have you seen an excellent Ashi Barai (foot sweep) executed without any follow-through? Renraku-Waza will make your technique instinctive, enabling you to follow through on every occasion with controlled power.

As with every aspect of karate, start slowly, building up your power and speed with every repetition. When possible, use a full length mirror, which is an invaluable aid.

Remember your goal is to put full power with focus (kime) into all your Waza (techniques), without it, you are wasting your time.

The combination techniques shown can obviously be practised in both stances and must be.

I have also chosen a distinctive background for the pictures in this chapter. This shows the techniques with perspective and also the distance covered when executing them.

A1 Start in left fighting stance (Hidari-Hanmi Gamae).

A2 Slide forward and punch with the leading hand (left fist) to the face.

A3 Punch right Gyakuzuki Chudan (reverse punch) remaining in left stance, pushing bodyweight forward.

A4 Quickly step up with right leg (Surikomi) without raising height too much and maintaining good balance keep hips at 45°

A5 Execute left Mawashigeri Jodan very fast (roundhouse kick to head).

A6 Place left leg down in front making sure that you are not shortening your stance and that you are still looking forward.

A7 Execute a right Ushirogeri (back kick) Chudan fast.

A8 Drop right leg down in front and execute a left Gyakuzuki Chudan fast.

A9 Pull fist back into right fighting stance (Migi-Hanmi Gamae).

B1 Right fighting stance (Migi-Hanmi Gamae).

B2 Step up with left leg, making sure not to raise body height and keep hips at 45°, (Surikomi).

B3 Kick right Maegeri Chudan.

B4 Snap kick back, do not place leg down.

B5 Twist hips through 90° preparing to deliver another kick.

B6 Execute right Mawashigeri Jodan (B3–B6 extremely fast combination).

B7 Place right leg down and strike right Uraken Jodan.

B8 Immediately follow up with a left Gyakuzuki Chudan.

B9 Return to Migi-Hanmi Gamae.

C1 Hidari-Hanmi Gamae.

C2 Step forward with the right leg and punch Migi Jodan Tsukki (right head punch).

C3 Step up with left leg (Surikomi).

C4 Execute a right side kick (Sokuto) to middle section (Chudan).

C5 Place right leg down and punch left Gyakuzuki Jodan.

C6 Finish in Migi-Hanmi Gamae.

D1 Hidari-Hanmi Gamae.

D2 Step up with the right leg (Surikomi).

D3 Kick Kingeri (Groin Kick) or to the upper thigh with the left leg.

D4 Snap leg back and raise left thigh.

D5 Kick Mawashigeri Jodan with left leg (D3–D5 very fast).

D6 Place left leg down and pull left fist back.

D7 Strike left Ukraken (back fist) Jodan.

D8 Immediately follow up with right Gyakuzuki Chudan

D9 *Pull fist back into left stance (Hidari-Hanmi Gamae).*

E1 *Hidari-Hanmi Gamae.*

E2 *Step up with right leg (Surikomi).*

E3 *Execute left Mawashigeri Chudan.*

17

E4 Place left leg down making sure to look over right shoulder (not taking eyes of opponent).

E5 Execute right Ushiro-Mawashigeri (back roundhouse kick) Jodan.

E6 Snap kick right back.

E7 Place right leg down and follow up with left Gyakuzuki Chudan.

E8 Finish in right stance.

F1 Hidari-Hanmi Gamae.

F2 Step up with right leg (Surikomi) pulling left fist back.

F3 Begin to strike out with left Uraken Jodan.

F4 Step forward with left leg and complete left Uraken strike.

F5 Pivot on left leg clockwise bringing right arm underneath left arm.

F6 Strike right Uraken Jodan.

F7 Finish in Migi-Hanmi Gamae.

G1 Hidari-Hanmi Gamae.

G2 Kick right Maegeri Chudan.

G3 Place right leg down directly in front.

G4 Punch right Jodan Tsukki (right face punch) and pull hips to the right (Nagashizuki) simultaneously.

G5 Pull right leg to the right and execute a left Gyakuzuki.

G6 Finish in right stance.

H1 Migi-Hanmi Gamae.

H2 Step up with left leg (Surikomi).

H3 Kick Sokuto Jodan with right leg.

H4 Place right leg down across body and look over left shoulder.

H5 Execute left Ushirogeri Chudan.

H6 Bring left leg down and execute a left Uraken Jodan.

H7 Follow up immediately with a right Gyakuzuki Chudan.

H8 Pull back into Hidari-Hanmi Gamae.

I1 Hidari-Hanmi Gamae.

I2 Step up with right leg (Surikomi).

I3 Execute a left Mawashigeri Jodan.

I4 Bring the left down and execute a left Ashibarai (leg sweep).

I5 Place left leg down in front and punch right Gyakuzuki.

I6 Hidari-Hanmi Gamae.

J1 Hidari-Hanmi Gamae.

J2 Step up with the right leg behind left leg making sure to keep focused on opponent.

J3 Bring left leg up preparing to execute a left Ura-Mawashigeri (hook kick).

J4 Execute a left Ura-Mawashigeri.

J5 Snap kick right back.

J6 Execute a left Mawashigeri Jodan.

J7 Place left leg down and strike a left Uraken Jodan.

J8 Follow up with a right Gyakuzuki Chudan.

J9 Pull fist back into left stance.

K1 Hidari-Hanmi Gamae.

K2 Swing right leg up executing a Mikazukigeri Chudan (right crescent kick – middle section

K3 Follow through with Mikazukigeri bringing right leg across body

K4 Without placing right foot down execute a Sokuto Fumikomi (side kick to the knee).

K5 Place right leg down and execute a left Gyakazuki Chudan.

K6 As left fist is pulled back execute a right Chudan Tsukki (stomach punch) using a powerful Hikite action (fist retraction and punch execution) at the same time pull left leg across with a Nagashi action.

K7 Pull right leg across and deliver a left Gyakuzuki Chudan.

K8 Pull left fist back into Migi-Hanmi Gamae.

CHAPTER II

Pairs

Pairwork is the way of keeping the fine edge on your karate technique.

Initially, many students do not like Ji-Yu Kumite (free fighting). It does not come naturally to the vast majority and should never be forced onto anyone. However, Ji-Yu Kumite is very important and must be practised once a student's confidence has been built up. By training with Yakusoku Kumite (pre-arranged pair techniques) regularly, then the ingredients for good Ji-Yu Kumite are practised. The major factors (in pair work) are good technique, timing, distance, speed, zanshin (awareness), accuracy, control and, above all, confidence. Pairs must be constantly repeated with varying speeds, ultimately concluding with full power attacks. Each attack and counter must be deliberate. Although the pairs are rehearsed, zanshin (awareness) must be present at all times. Lack of concentration can result in serious injury and is quite common in an undisciplined Dojo (training hall).

Not only are the physical techniques being polished, but so is the mind with total concentration. Both body and mind are training for the ultimate test of combat, but by training diligently, one strives to be strong enough to walk away from a confrontation.

Obviously, should a situation occur where it becomes impossible to avoid using your karate, I personally believe that unless you have practised actual fighting in the dojo, then your chances of coming out on top are

約束組手

minimal. I know some schools advocate that free fighting and competition is far too dangerous, but I totally disagree.

Quite often when a senior graded karate-ka sustains an injury, and is unable to do any Ji-Yu Kumite, he will practice pairs in order to keep his technique sharp, in the same way a novice strives to get sharp technique. Also, at a certain age a karate-ka may decide he no longer wishes to participate in kumite and can therefore increase his pairwork practice.

In this section I have selected quite a few pair techniques for demonstration. Always practice both attack and defence in both stances with different partners of differing build and height. Like Ji-Yu Kumite practice, the more varied the opponent, the more challenging the training becomes. Eventually, your reactions will be instinctive, enabling you to meet any attack and counter successfully.

Always ensure that your distance is correct when practising pairwork. One Surikomi's distance is a good guide.

"Karate begins and finishes with courtesy" *(Funakoshi)*. The famous saying is emphasised in pairwork practice. Before each attack, both you and your partner must bow and again at the end of each attack.

The pairs are shown in two sections: Offensive techniques and Defense techniques.

Attacks

A1 Both in left.

A2 Attacker slides forwards and punches left fist to the face. Opponent leans back to avoid punch.

A3 Attacker immediately punches right Gyakuzuki Chudan.

A4 Both pull back into right stance.

B1 Attacker right, Defender left.

B2 Attacker kicks left leg to the groin (Kingeri).

B3 Attacker immediately grabs opponent's ears and drives a right Hizageri into the face (knee kick).

B4 Attacker left, Defender right.

C1 Attacker left, Defender right.

C2 Attacker kicks right Mikazuki Geri (crescent kick) knocking opponent's leading arm out.

C3 Attacker snaps leg back.

C4 Attacker kicks right Sokuto Chudan (side kick).

C5 Both pull back into left stance.

D1 Face each other.

D2 Rei. (Bow).

D3 Attacker left, Defender right.

D4 Attacker slides in with the left leg and pushes opponent's front guard down, immediately swing right leg around in a clockwise direction.

D5 Continue pivoting around on the left leg and strike Uraken Jodan with right first to opponent's temple at the same time covering his leading arm with your left hand.

D6 Both spin back into left stance, and then Rei.

E1 Face each other.

E2 Rei.

E3 Attacker left, Defender right.

E4 Attacker slides in with the left leg and pushes opponent's front guard down, immediately swing right leg around in a clockwise direction.

E5 Continue swinging right leg around fast and break opponent's balance by striking his front leg.

E6 Cover opponent's front arm and punch left Gyakuzuki to his back. Attacker steps back with right leg into left. Opponent spins out into left stance. Rei.

F1 Both in right stance.

F2 Attacker steps up with his left leg behind his right at the same time pushes opponent's guard down with right backhand (Haisho).

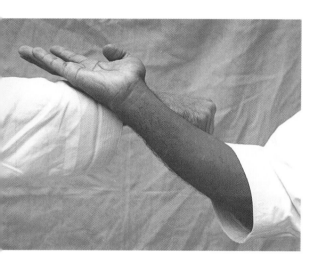

F3 Keep opponent's front arm down and kick the back of his right calf with the right foot.

F4 Change the right hand block to a grab of opponent's right wrist and kick with your right foot to opponent's head.

F5 Both step back into left stance.

G1 Both in right stance.

G2 Attacker kicks left Mawashigeri Jodan.

G3 Without placing left leg down on floor, drop it down fast and sweep opponent's front leg with an Ashi Barai covering opponent's front arm.

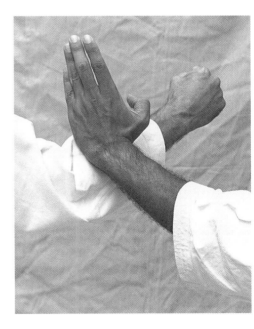

G4 Immediately punch right Gyakuzuki to opponent's kidney.

G5 Both pull back. Attacker in right stance, Opponent in left.

H1 Attacker left, Defender right.

H2 Attacker steps forwards and pushes opponent's right arm down with his right Shuto (knife hand).

H3 Attacker steps up with his left leg and sweeps opponent's right leg with his right leg.

H4 When opponent's balance has been broken, Attacker raises right knee.

H5 Attacker kicks right Mawashigeri Jodan.

H6 Both step back into left stance.

I1 Both in right stance.

I2 Attacker sweeps opponent's right leg with his left leg (Ashibarai), cover opponent's guard with left hand.

I3 Immediately punch to opponent's ribs with right Gyakuzuki.

I4 Attacker raises right leg and kicks Sokuto to opponent's right leg at the knee joint

I5 Attacker punches opponent in the back of the head.

I6 Both pull back into left stance.

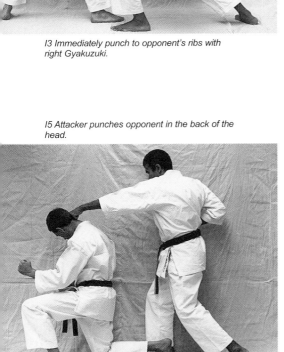

J1 Both in left stance, then Attacker steps forward with his right leg (Surikomi).

J2 Attacker kicks left Sokuto Chudan, placing left leg down in front. Opponent takes one pace backwards to avoid kick.

J3 Defender takes one step forward with his left leg preparing to counter kick with his right leg. Attacker immediately steps forward diagonally with his right leg crossing path of Attacker and prepares to deliver a right Haito (ridge hand) Chudan.

J4 Defender delivers a right Maegeri as Attacker strikes haito and then grabs opponent around the waist breaking his balance.

J6 Throwing him onto the ground, punch with the right fist into back of the head.

J5 Attacker completely throws opponent over his hips.

J7 Both back into left stance.

K1 Both in right stance.

K2 Attacker steps forward and punches to opponent's face with left fist. Opponent takes one pace backwards.

K3 Attacker kicks with the right leg, Sokuto Jodan. Opponent takes one step back.

K4 Opponent immediately counters by stepping forward with his left leg and punches with his left fist to Attacker's face. Attacker side-steps with his right leg into left Neko-Ashi-Dachi and blocks the punch with a right Uchi Uke.

K5 Attacker grabs opponent's left wrist with is left hand and strikes right Shuto (knife hand) to opponent's throat.

K6 Attacker pulls opponent with left arm sliding his right forearm against opponent's throat until his elbow is on the throat. Attacker is now in Shiko Dachi.

K7 Attacker drops his body weight as low as he can possibly go whilst still pres[s] on opponent's throat with his right elbow and pulling opponent's left arm acros[s] body against the elbow joint.

K8 Attacker falls backwards pulling opponent with him (MAKE SURE YOU RELEASE TENSION ON OPPONENT'S LEFT ARM AND ALSO PULL RIGHT ELBOW OUT OF OPPONENT'S THROAT AS YOU LAND).

K9 Attacker brings left leg over and kicks opponent in groin with heel of left foot

K10 Both peel away from each other, and return to......

K11 Attacker Left, Defender Right.

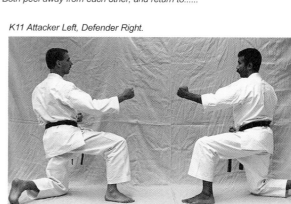

Counter-Attack

L1 Both in left stance.

L2 Attacker throws a right Gyakuzuki to the face (Jodan).
Defender slides forward with his left leg and pulls body to
the left (Taisabaki) executing a left punch to the face and
parrying Attacker's punch with the right back hand (Haisho).

L3 Pull back, Attacker in right, Defender in right.

M1 Attacker left, Defender right.

M2 Attacker kicks right Mawashigeri Chudan. Defender slides forward with his right leg executing Taisabaki grabbing the kick underneath with is left arm and immediately striking Uraken to Attacker's groin.

M3 Both pull back into left stance.

N1 Attacker left, Defender right.

N2 Attacker punches right Gyakuzuki Chudan, Defender pulls body weight back and pushes Attacker's punch down with a left Teisho (palm heel) block.

N3 Defender pushes his body weight forward and punches Attacker in the face with a right Seiken.

N4 Both pull back. Attacker in right, Defender in left.

O1 Both in right stance.

O2 Attacker steps forward and punches with his left fist to the face. Defender raises left arm and pushes the Attacker's arm downwards whilst sliding right leg forward and delivering a right punch to the Attacker's left rib cage.

O3 Defender immediately grabs the left wrist of the Attacker pulling him down and delivering a left (Hiza-geri) knee kick to the body.

O4 Both step back into right stance.

P1 Both in right stance.

P2 Attacker steps forwards and tries to strike left Uraken to the head (back fist). Defender steps back and blocks left Jodan Uke.

P3 Defender immediately pivots on his left foot and executes a right Ushirogeri-Chudan (back kick to the stomach).

P4 Attacker right, Defender left. (Step back).

Q1 Both in left stance.

Q2 Attacker begins to throw out a right Gyakuzuki.

Q3 Defender drops down onto right knee and blocks with a left Jodan Uke, simultaneously punching right Gyakuzuki Chudan to Attacker.

Q4 Both step back into right stance.

50

R1 Both in left stance, then

▲ R2 Attacker begins to throw out a right Gyakuzuki. Defender quickly shuffles legs changing stance and blocks Attacker's punch with his left arm, preparing to strike right Uraken.

▶R3 Defender strikes right Uraken, then pulls back into opposite stance, Attacker in right and Defender in left.

S1 Face each other, then Rei (bow) to each other.

S2 Both in left stance. Attacker always moves forward fractionally before defender steps back.

▲ *S3 Attacker steps forward with a lunge punch to the middle section (Chudan). Defender pulls his right foot to the left keeping his left foot still pivoting on it. (Taisabaki) (Hip shifting Technique). Simultaneously punch with left fist to the face.*

▼ *S5 Both pull away from each other extremely fast. Attacker in left stance, Defender in right stance.*

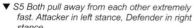

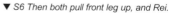

▲ *S4 Cover the attacker's punching arm with your left arm and follow up with a right Gyakuzuki (reverse punch) Chudan.*

▼ *S6 Then both pull front leg up, and Rei.*

T1 Face each other, Rei, Attacker left stance, Defender right stance.

▲ T2 Attacker kicks with right Mawashigeri Chudan. Defender blocks with left Heisho and slides in punching with right fist to face.

▶ T3 As Attacker places his right foot down, Defender twists hips and strikes left elbow (Empi-uchi) to the face. Both pull pack into left stance. Rei.

◄ U1 Face each other. Rei. Attacker kicks right Maegeri Chudan, Defender pulls left leg over to his right pivoting on right foot (Taisabaki) and prepares to block with right hand by swinging it out to the right.

◄ U2 Defender pushes kick outwards

◄ U3 Defender counters with a right back fist strike (Uraken Uchi) to Attacker's temple.

◄ U4 Defender immediately follows up with a left Gyakuzuki Chudan. Both step back into left stance. Rei.

◀ V1 Both in left. Attacker kicks right Maegeri Chudan, Defender slides forward with his left leg and scoops the kicking leg underneath in an anti-clockwise move – Mawashi-Uke.

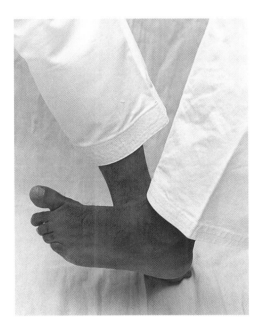

▲ V2 Defender steps forward with his right leg and grabs Attacker's collar with his left hand.

▲ V3 Defender pulls hard on the collar, lifts Attacker's leg higher with his right arm and sweeps Attacker's supporting leg away with his left leg.

V4 As soon as Attacker is down, Defender punches Attacker in the temple. Defender does not let go of the collar whilst dropping Attacker and pins him with his right knee once he is down, then both pull back into right stance.

W1

W1 Face each other. Rei. Attacker left, Defender right.. Attacker kicks right Sokuto Chudan. Defender jumps to the left blocking the Sokuto with a right Gedan Barai.

W2 Defender grabs Attacker's right wrist with his right hand and punches Attacker in the side of the neck with his left fist.

W3 Defender grabs Attacker's collar with his left hand and gets a good grip of Attacker's right sleeve.

W4 Defender pulls Attacker backwards with his left arm and sweeps Attacker's right foot forwards with his left foot.

W5 Drop Attacker down in front without letting go of collar and finish off with a right Seiken (straight punch) to the temple.

W6 Defender steps back with his left leg into right stance, Attacker brings his right leg over going over onto his right knee. Rei.

W2

W3

W5

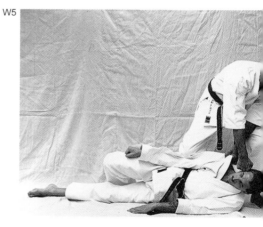

W4

W6

56

X1 Face each other
   Rei.
   Attacker left, Defender right.

X2 Attacker punches Gyakuzuki Chudan with his
   right fist. Defender pulls weight back into
   right Neko Ashi Dachi and blocks punch with
   left Teisho Uke (palm heel block).

X3 Attacker punches with the left fist to the face.
   Defender pushes his weight forward and
   blocks the punch with a right Uchi-Uke
   (inside block) Jodan.

X4 The Attacker kicks right Maegeri to
   Defender's stomach. Defender pivots
   clockwise on his left leg doing a complete
   circle with the right leg and prepares to block.

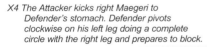

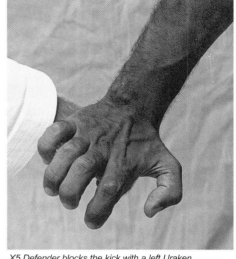

X5 Defender blocks the kick with a left Uraken
   Uke (back fist block) using the momentum of
   the spin to push the kick away.

X6 Defender continues to raise the Uraken block then swings it down as a Uraken Uchi (strike) to the Attacker's ribs as he lands.

X7 Defender shifts weight of the left striking right Teisho (palm heel) to Attacker's right kidney.

X8 Defender places left hand on top of Attacker's head and cups his right hand under Attacker's jaw and begins to twist head whilst moving clockwise.

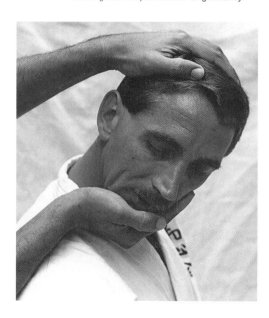

X9 Continue moving clockwise around the Attacker, twisting his head downwards and force him to the ground.

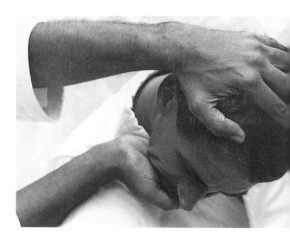

X10 As soon as Attacker is down raise right foot to stamp on him.

X11 Stamp Fumikomi to body.

X12

CHAPTER III

Kata

The katas shown are all connected with the Shuri and the Tomari Region of Okinawa. I have selected them not only because of their fast and rapid technique, which is characteristic of Shuri-Te Karate, but also due to their heavy Chinese influence, which is still quite apparent. There is strong evidence that a form of Kata, more like a dance, existed in Okinawa, long before China had a controlling influence.

When looking at different Chinese systems and training with Chinese Martial Arts Instructors, it is quite obvious that there are great similarities in both execution of technique and application. It is a known fact that Okinawan-Te was greatly influenced by the Chinese military fighting systems.

Modern karate-do still has Kata as its backbone.

Kata is the life and soul of karate. If you do not practice kata, then you are not studying the true art of karate-do. In kata training, you strive to focus the mind on imaginary attacks and counter-attacks and simultaneously let the body carry out the physical actions making the mind and body one.

The kata selected are personal favourites. Kata must be practised regularly and correctly. Advanced kata are practised in exactly the same way as basic kata, methodically and deliberately and completely learning the subject matter.

As well as picking up the physical techniques, it is often useful to learn the history of a kata, if at all possible. The Bunkai (application) is extremely important and the kata cannot be understood if the Bunkai is not explained. As stated in my previous book, practise kata initially slowly until confidence is gained. Then apply speed and power to your technique. Concentrate on the rhythm of the movements, making sure the combinations are fast and powerful and the slow movements are deliberate and purposeful.

In the captions underneath the pictures, I have shown where these changes of rhythm take place.

Always remember that the kata illustrated in this book are guides and will aid your karate training, but you can never learn kata only from a book. There is absolutely no substitute for a good Sensei (teacher) who can help inspire good performance and motivate you with good, clear instruction. Also, without good regular instruction, there is always the tendency to improvise when uncertain about the next move in a kata and this can establish a pattern of errors which can then become ingrained. This, unfortunately, happens far too often and has seen the loss of many of the true movements of many historical kata.

Trying to get the feeling of satisfaction with every performance of a kata is rare, if not impossible. One out of every 20 is usually the case, even when that particular kata is well known to you.

Bassai

1 Yoi.

2 Step forward with right leg, swinging both arms to the left, keeping right fist pressed into open left palm.

3 Block Migi Soto Uke Jodan reinforced with the left arm, stepping into Gyaku Neko Ashi Dachi, fast.

4 Step behind with the left leg into Hidari Sanchin Dachi (left hour glass stance) and perform Hidari Soto Uke Jodan, fast.

4a Rear View

5 Block Migi Soto Uke Jodan fast

5a Rear View.

6 Step across with the right leg behind, pivoting 180 degrees, facing the front, into Migi Neko Ashi Dachi and execute Hidari Uchi Uke Jodan, fast.

7 Execute Migi Soto Uke Jodan, fast.

8 Swing right leg to the right, dropping height as body twists 90 degrees and do a scooping block with the right arm, fast.

9 Raise height back into Migi Neko Ashi Dachi, bringing right arm up Jodan height (8 and 9 one continuous move, fast).

10 Block Migi Uchi Uke Jodan, fast.

11 Block Hidari Soto Uke Jodan, fast.

12 Twist body 90 degrees into Shizentai (Mashomen), bringing left arm across body, slow.

13 Execute Hidari Gedan Barai, fast.

14 Execute Migi Chudan Tsuki, fast.

15 Step out to the left with the left leg and block Soto Uke Jodan, rotating hip 90 degrees, fast.

16 Pull left leg up into Shizentai Dachi and execute a fast Hidari Chudan Tsuki.

17 Step to the right with the right leg and execute Hidari Soto Uke Jodan, twisting the hips through 90 degrees, fast.

18 Pull left leg in halfway, stepping directly in front with the right leg, placing left hand out in front and cupping right hand behind left ear, fast.

19 Execute Migi Shuto Uke, fast.

20 Step forward into Hidari Neko Ashi Dachi and perform Hidari Shuto Uke, fast.

21 Step forward into Migi Neko Ashi Dachi and perform Migi Shuto Uke, fast.

22 Step back with right leg into Hidari Neko Ashi Dachi, crossing right hand over left, fast.

23 Execute Hidari Kake Uke Chudan and Migi Teisho Uke Chudan, fast.

24 Transfer weight onto left leg, Gyaku Neko Ashi Dachi, rotating upper body 90 degrees, grabbing opponent's forearm and wrist, fast.

25 Pull both arms behind you and kick Migi Sokuto Fumikomi, fast, Kiai.

26 Step down to the front with kicking leg and pivot 180 degrees behind, performing Hidari Shuto Uke in Hidari Neko Ashi Dachi, fast.

26a Rear View

27 Step forward into Migi Neko Ashi Dachi, executing Migi Shuto Uke, fast.

27a Rear View.

28 Pull right leg back, dropping both arms downwards, slowly.

28a Rear View.

29 Right foot comes into Musubi Dachi, both fists raised above the head, slowly.

30 Step forward with right leg into Migi Zenkutsu Dachi and execute double tettsui Uchi Chudan, fast.

30a Rear View.

31 Without changing stance, execute a powerful Migi Chudan Tsuki.

31a Rear View.

32 Pull left leg up to meet the right leg into Musubi Dachi, twisting body 90 degrees. Look directly in front, executing Hidari Gedan Barai and Migi Soto Uke Jodan, fast.

32a Rear View.

33 Step to the front with the right leg into Shiko Dachi and execute Migi Tettsu Uchi Chudan, fast.

33a Side View.

34 Raise both arms above the head, pulling the left leg up into Shizentai Dachi and execute Hidari Tettsui Uchi Chudan in the opposite direction, fast.

34a Side View.

35 Swing right leg up executing Mikuzuki Geri Chudan, striking palm of open left hand.

35a Side View.

36 Drop right leg into Shiko Dachi and execute Migi Empi Uchi Chudan, looking to the right, fast.

36a Rear View.

36b Front Side view.

37 Execute Morote Gedan Barai to the right, fast.

37a Side View.

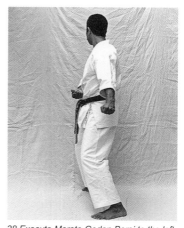

38 Execute Morote Gedan Barai to the left, remain looking to the right, fast.

38a Side View.

39 Execute Migi Gedan Barai to the right, looking to the right, fast..

39a Side View.

40 Pull right leg in, tucking right elbow into side, slowly. (Side view).

41 Slide forward with right leg into Junzuki No Tsukkomi and execute Yama Tsuki, fast.

41a Side View.

42 Pull right leg back into Musubi Dachi, bringing left arm across body, right fist on hip, medium speed.

42a Side View.

43 Slide forward with left leg into Junzuki No Tsukkomi and execute Yama Tsuki, fast.

43a Side View.

44 Bring left leg back into Musubi Dachi, bringing right arm across the body, left fist on hip, medium speed.

44a Side View.

45 Slide forward with right leg into Junzuki No Tsukkomi and execute Yama Tsuki, fast.

45a Side View.

46 Step across 90 degrees behind with the left leg, twisting body 180 degrees in Gyakuzuki No Tsukkomi Dachi, executing Migi Soto Uke Jodan, twisting hips 90 degrees, fast.

47 Step in and out the right leg into Migi Gyakuzuki No Tsukkomi, executing Hidari Soto Uke Jodan, twisting hips through 90 degrees, fast.

48 Step in with the left leg, dropping left arm in front bringing right arm up behind left ear, fast and slide right leg forward.

49 In Migi Neko Ashi Dachi, execute a slow Jodan Shuto Uke.

50 Remain looking in front, rotate right hip 135 degrees to the right into Migi Neko Ashi Dachi, dropping both hands down to the left, fast.

51 Remain looking in front, execute slow Migi Shuto Uke Jodan in direction of stance.

52 Still looking in front, drop hands down, step up with the right leg past left leg and step forward with left leg into Hidari Neko Ashi Dachi, 180 degrees from previous stance, fast.

53 Still looking directly in front, execute a slow Hidari Jodan Shuto Uke in direction of stance.

54 Twist right foot and pull left foot back into Heisoku Dachi (Yame).

Wanshu

1 Rei.

2 Yoi: Press right fist into open left palm on the left side of body, Heisoku Dachi.

3 Step to the left with left leg and execute Gedan Tsuki with right fist to left side, fast.

4 Look right and bring right arm across the body, fast.

5 Execute Migi Gedan Barai, fast.

6 Execute Hidari Chudan Tsuki, across body, fast, bringing right fist into hip.

7 Step forward with left leg into Hidari Zenkutsu Dachi and perform Hidari Gedan Barai, fast.

8 Execute Migi Jodan Gyakuzuki, fast.

9 Keep arms in position and execute Migi Maegeri Chudan, fast

10 Place right leg down in front, dropping weight and execute Hidari Gedan Tsuki, bringing right arm across chest, fast.

11 Step back with left leg into Migi Zenkutsu Dachi and perform Migi Gedan Barai, fast.

12 Pull left leg across behind into Hidari Zenkutsu Dachi and perform Hidari Gedan Barai, fast.

12a Reverse view.

13 Execute Migi Jodan Gyakuzuki, fast.

14 Keep arms in position and execute Migi Maegeri Chudan, fast.

15 Place right leg down in front, dropping weight and execute Hidari Gedan Tsukki, bringing right arm across chest, fast.

16 Step back with left leg into Migi Zenkutsu Dachi and perform Migi Gedan Barai, fast.

17 Pull left leg across, turning 180 degrees into Hidari Zenkutsu Dachi and perform left Gedan Barai, fast.

18 Bring right hand out 90 degrees to the body, keeping fist clenched and bring left hand out 90 degrees, opening hand.

19 Bring both hands p above head in a circular motion and strike the palm of the open left hand with Migi Tettsui.

20/20a Bring hands down in front of body and execute Migi Sokuto Chudan, fast, Kiai.

21 Place right leg down to the right into Shiko Dachi and execute Hidari Jodan Shuto Uke, fast.

22 Punch Migi Chudan Tsuki, fast.

23 Punch Hidari Chudan Tsuki, fast.

24 Move left leg back twisting hips 90 degrees to the left into Hidari Zenkutsu Dachi and perform Hidari Gedan Barai, fast.

25 Punch Migi Gyakuzuki Chudan, fast.

26 Step forward with right leg into Migi Neko Ashi Dachi, swing arms to the left, preparing to block, fast.

27 Execute Migi Jodan Shuto Uke, fast.

28 Pull right leg back into Neko Ashi Dachi Sho.

28a Step forward with left leg into Hidari Neko Ashi Dachi, swing arms to the right.

29 Execute Hidari Shuto Uke, fast.

30 Execute Migi Gyakuzuki Chudan, fast.

31 Pull left leg back into Neko Ashi Dachi Sho.

31a As 26.

32 Execute Migi Jodan Shuto Uke, fast.

33 Pull left leg across 180 degrees, preparing to turn, left arm across chest, fast.

34 Step down with left leg into Hidari Zenkutsu Dachi and perform Hidari Gedan Barai.

35 Punch Migi Gyakuzuki Jodan, fast.

36 Kick Migi Maegeri Chudan, keeping arms in position, fast

37 Place right leg down in front, dropping weight and execute Hidari Gedan Tsuki, bringing right arm across chest fast (Kiai).

38 Step back with left leg into Migi Zenkutsu Dachi and perform Migi Gedan Barai, fast.

39 Pull left leg across behind turning 180 degrees into Hidari Zenkutsu Dachi and perform Hidari Gedan Barai, fast.

40 Raise left arm out in front Jodan height and drop right arm behind opening both hands, fast.

41 Block directly in front Teisho Uke Chudan, pulling left fist on to hip, fast.

42 Twist hips 90 degrees to front (Mashomen) and step forward with right leg, fast.

43 Step down with right leg into Migi Zenkutsu Dachi and perform rising Migi Teisho Uke and dropping Hidari Teisho Uke Gedan, fast.

44 Step forward with left leg, rotating wrists, fast.

45 Step down with left leg into Hidari Zenkutsu Dachi, and perform rising Hidari Teisho Uke and dropping Migi Teisho Uke Gedan, fast.

46 Step forward with right leg rotating both wrists, fast.

47 Step forward with right leg into Migi Zenkutsu Dachi and perform rising Migi Teisho Uke and dropping Hidari Teisho Uke Gedan, fast.

48 Raise arms crossing right arm in front of left.

48a Block Migi Gedan Barai (fast).

49 Retract right leg pulling right arm in and execute Migi Yama Tsukki in Migi Junzuki No Tsukkomi, fast.

49a Open both hands.

50 Swing right leg round and up fast, preparing to jump.

51 Execute Tobi Shuto Uke through 360 degrees.

52 Land in Migi Neko Ashi Dachi, left arm in front, right arm behind left ear, fast.

53 Execute Migi Jodan Shuto Uke, fast.

54 Step back with right leg into Hidari Neko Ashi Dachi and perform Hidari Shuto Uke Jodan, fast.

55 Twist right foot, pull left leg back into Heisoku Dachi, right arm across body, pressing into open left palm, left side of the body (Yame).

56 Rei.

1 Musubi Dachi.

2 Heisoku Dachi, right fist pressed into open left hand.

3 Step back with left leg into Migi Zenkutsu Dachi and execute Hidari Gedan Barai and Migi Soto Uke Jodan, fast.

4 Step up with left leg into Musubi Dachi, looking right, fast.

5 Step to the left with the left leg into Kokotsu Dachi, looking to the right, block Hidari Soto Uke Jodan and Migi Gedan Barai, fast.

6 Transfer weight into Migi Kokotsu Dachi, looking to the left, blocking Hidari Gedan Barai and Migi Soto Uke Jodan, fast.

7 Move left leg to the left into Hidari Zenkutsu Dachi and execute Hidari Jodan Uke, fast.

8 Step forward and punch Migi Junzuki Chudan, fast.

9 Bring right leg behind, crossing right arm across chest, fast.

10 Pivot 180 degrees into Migi Zenkutsu Dachi and execute Migi Jodan Uke, fast.

11 Step forward with left leg and execute Hidari Junzuki Chudan, fast.

12 Pull left leg back into Musubi Dachi, crossing left arm in front of right at chest level, slowly, and look left.

13 Step out with the left leg directly in front into Shiko Dachi and strike Tettsui (bottom fist) Chudan.

14 Move left leg to the left, shoulders and hips square to the front and open hands.

15 Step forward with right leg into Shiko Dachi and execute rising Teisho with right hand and downward Teisho with left hand, Chudan level, keep looking directly in front (Numbers 14 and 15 executed fast).

16 Move right leg to the right, squaring the shoulders and hips to the front and rotate both hands 180 degrees.

17 Step forward with the left leg into Shiko Dachi, executing a rising Hidari Teisho Uke and a downward Migi Teisho Uke, Chudan level (16 & 17 executed fast).

18 Still looking in front move left leg to the left, shoulders and hips square to the front and rotate hands 180 degrees.

19 Step forward with right leg into Shiko Dachi and execute rising Teisho with right hand and downward Teisho with left hand, Chudan level, keep looking directly in front and Kiai.

20 Pivot behind 225 degrees and into Hidari Neko Ashi, bringing open left hand up in front of right open hand, fast.

20a Picture in reverse.

21 Slowly clench fists and pull arms apart, shoulder width.

21a Picture in reverse.

22 Pull both hands back on to the hips fast and execute Migi Maegeri Chudan, fast.

22a Picture in reverse.

23 Place right foot down in front into Migi Zenkutsu Dachi and execute Migi Chudan Tsuki, fast.

23a Reverse picture.

24 Execute Hidari Gyakuzuki Chudan, fast.

24a Picture in reverse.

25 Execute Hidari Gedan Barai and Migi Soto Uke Jodan, fast.

25a Picture in reverse.

26 Pivot 90 degrees to the right into Migi Neko Ashi Dachi, bringing right open hand up in front of left open hand, chest height, fast.

26a Picture in reverse

27 Slowly perform wedge block, clenching fists, shoulder width.

27a Picture in reverse.

28 Pull both fists back on to hip and execute hidari Maegeri Chudan, fast.

91

28a Picture in reverse.

29 Step down with left leg into Zenkutsu Dachi and execute hidari Chudan Tsuki, fast.

29a Picture in reverse.

30 Execute Migi Gyakuzuki Chudan, fast.

30a Picture in reverse.

31 Execute Migi Gedan Barai, Hidari Soto Uke Jodan, fast.

31a Picture in reverse.

32 Look over left shoulder and step clockwise with the right leg, bringing right hand underneath left.

32a Picture in reverse.

33 Continue circle landing in Shiko Dachi and execute Migi Tettsui Uchi Chudan, fast.

33a Picture in reverse.

34 Bring left leg around in an anti-clockwise direction, bringing left hand underneath right hand.

34a Picture in reverse.

35 Continue circle landing in Shiko Dachi and execute Hidari Tettsui Uchi Chudan, fast.

35a Side view.

36 Pull left leg back into Musubi Dachi, squaring hips and shoulders 90 degrees to the rear, crossing left hand in front of right, chest level, fast.

36a Picture in reverse.

37 Step out to the left with the left leg into Shiko Dachi and block Hidari Gedan Barai, fast.

37a Picture in reverse.

38 Punch Migi Chudan Tsuki across body with right fist, fast, do not overtwist shoulders.

38a Picture in reverse.

39 Execute Hidari Chudan Tsuki, remaining in Shiko Dachi, fast.

39a Picture in reverse.

40 Step across behind with left leg bringing right arm underneath left.

41 Land in Shiko Dachi, Mashomen (facing front) and execute Hidari Gedan Barai and right Soto Uke Jodan, shoulder width, fast.

42 Bring the right arm down across the body in front of the Gedan Barai, slowly, until both arms are parallel.

43 Bring both hands up together touching fists at Chudan height and continue rising up pressing forearms together, Jodan height, slow.

44 Pull arms apart, wedge block, slowly, shoulder width.

45 Execute Migi Jodan Kizamazuki (Jodan snap punch), Kiai.

46 Continue Kiai as you execute Hidari. Kizamazuki, fast.

47 Pivot on right foot to the left into Hidari Zenkutsu Dachi and block Hidari Jodan Uke, fast.

48 Step forward and execute Migi Junzuki.

49 Pull back with right leg bringing right arm across chest.

50 Step down with the right leg into right Zenkutsu Dachi and execute right Jodan Uke.

51 Execute Hidari Junzuki, fast.

52 Pull left leg behind and pull right leg up.

53 Heisoku Dachi.   *54 Rei.*

ROHAI (TOMARI)

1 Attention Stance (Musubi Dachi).

2 Bow (Rei.)

3 Step out to the left with the left leg, raising both hands upwards in a circular motion (Yoi).

4 Cross left hand over right and bring down sharply directly in front of the body, keeping both palms parallel and shoulder width.

5 Pull to the right into Shiko Dachi fast, blocking Shuto Uke Gedan.

6 Twist to the left 180 degrees into Neko Ashi Dachi, blocking Hidari Kake Chudan, pulling right fist back on to hip, slow.

7 Remain in Neko Ashi Dachi, punch Migi Gyakuzuki fast, pulling left fist on to hip, shoulders mashomen to attack.

8 Pull right heel up to left heel, Musubi Dachi, twisting body 90 degrees to the front, Shomen, pulling right fist on to hip, slow.

9 Take a natural step forward with the left leg, slowly.

10 Take a natural step forward with the right leg, slowly.

11 Step back with the left leg, raising right hand above head and left hand across stomach, both hands open. Quickly.

12 Raise right leg into Sagi Ashi Dachi simultaneously block down with right hand Teisho and bring back of left hand across face, Heisho Uke.

13 Still in Sagi Ashi Dachi, swing both arms palms down to the left, fast.

14 Pivot 45 degrees to the right landing in Migi Junzuki stance (Migi Zenkutsu Dachi) blocking Morote Migi Haito Uke (right ridge hand) Chudan.

15 Rotate Migi Haito into Migi Kake, slowly.

16 Step forward and punch Hidari Junzuki, Hidari Zenkutsu Dachi, fast.

17 Punch on the spot Migi Gyakuzuki Chudan, fast.

18 Step back with the left leg diagonally and do a scooping action upwards with the left arm.

19 Landing in Shiko Dachi, punch Seiken Gedan bringing left fist across chest, fast.

20 Step back with left leg, raising right arm above head, left arm across stomach.

21 Pull right leg up behind left leg into Sagi Ashi Dachi, blocking Migi Teisho Uke, bringing left hand across face.

22 Step down 45 degrees to the left with the right leg into Migi Zenkutsu Dachi and block Morote Migi Haito Uke, fast.

23 Without changing stance, rotate wrist and perform kake, slow.

24 Step forward and punch Hidari Junzuki Chudan, fast.

25 Without changing stance, punch Gyakuzuki Chudan, fast.

26 Twist body 45 degrees to the right and step forward Shomen facing front, executing double palm heel strike Chudan, fast and Kiai.

27 Step back with left leg raising right hand above head left arm across body.

28 Bring right leg up behind left leg into Sagi Ashi Dachi blocking Migi Teisho Uke and bringing left hand up to protect face, fast.

29 Step down directly in front, Shomen, blocking Migi Haito Uke, reinforced, fast.

30 Rotate right wrist, performing Kake, slowly.

31 Step forward punch Hidari Junzuki Chudan, fast.

32 Punch Gyakuzuki on the spot, Chudan, fast.

33 Slowly pull left leg back into Musubi Dachi and bring left arm across body.

34 Slide left leg forward into Junzuki No Tsukkomi Dachi and perform double punch, Yama Tsuki, fast.

35 Slowly pull left leg back, bringing right arm across body.

36 Slide forward with right leg into Junzuki No Tsukkomi Dachi and perform Yama Tsuki, fast.

37 Pull right leg back slowly bringing left arm across the body.

38 Slide left leg forward into Junzuki No Tsukkomi Dachi and perform Yama Tsuki, fast.

39 Bring right hand down in a scooping motion, Chudan level, and left hand up behind right ear, fast.

40 Pull weight completely back into Hidari Neko Ashi Dachi and perform Hidari Shuto Uke.

41 Extend left hand and execute Migi Mikazuki Geri Chudan level, fast.

41a Side view.

42 Continue to circle around anti-clockwise behind the body.

43 Continue to pivot on the right leg so the left leg spirals around the right in an anti-clockwise motion, bringing the left hand underneath the right, fast.

44 Transfer the weight on to the left leg and perform Shuto Uke with the right hand. Migi Neko Ashi Dachi.

45 Step back with the right leg into Neko Ashi Dachi and perform Shuto Uke with the left hand, fast.

46 Pull left leg back, preparing to finish, at the same time, bring left hand on top of right in a circular motion.

47 Yame.

48 Rei.

1 Yoi.

2 Slide right leg forward, bringing right arm across to the left, placing back of the right elbow on the back of the left wrist.

3 Step down in to Migi Junzuki stance and do a pressing block with the left open hand, pushing the Migi uraken out, slow and deliberate.

4 Step forward with the left leg and then off at 45 degrees to the left, fast, into Neko Ashi Dachi, bringing left open hand up underneath right open hand, fast.

5 Push both hands apart performing a wedge block, slowly and deliberately.

6 Step in and out 90 degrees with the right leg, bringing right hand up underneath left, fast.

7 Do a wedge block with both hands, slowly.

8 Step up with left leg, fast, keeping same height, look left 90 degrees and bring left hand underneath right armpit, left open hand, extending right fist in direction facing.

9 Slowly step out 90 degrees to the left, performing Hidari Kake Uke, pulling right fist back on to hip. The move is executed slowly with all limbs stopping at the same time.

10 Execute Migi Gyakuzuki Chudan, fast.

11 Execute hidari Chudan Tsuki, fast.

12 Execute Migi Maegeri Chudan, fast.

13 Snap kick and bring back into Hidari Junzuki stance, fast.

14 Perform Gyakuzuki Chudan, fast.

15 Pull right leg up to left leg, looking 90 degrees to the right, bringing open right hand underneath left armpit and extending left punch in direction of attack, quickly.

16 Step out to the right 90 degrees with the right leg into Neko Ashi Dachi, performing Migi Kake Uke, pulling left fist on to hip. Slowly and deliberately.

17 Punch Gyakuzuki Chudan with the left fist, fast.

18 Punch Migi Chudan Tsuki.

109

19 Kick Maegeri Chudan with the left leg, fast.

20 Snap back and place down into Migi Zenkutsu Dachi

21 Punch Hidari Gyakuzuki Chudan, fast.

22 Step to the front with the right leg into Junzuki No Tsukkomi Dachi and strike upwards Migi Jodan Empi.

23 Begin to pivot 180 degrees bringing Migi Yonhon Nukite (spearhead) on top of left back hand.

23a Complete pivot of 180 degrees into Hidari neko Ashi Dachi, bringing hands down in front of the body (and then pull to the right). Slowly and deliberately.

23b Here picture reversed. (Sequence shown from rear direction).

24 Step forward with right leg into Migi Neko Ashi Dachi and execute Migi Jodan Shuto Uke, fast. (Neko Ashi Dachi).

25 Pull back right leg into Heisoku Dachi and execute Hidari Chudan Yonhon Nukite, fast.

26 Step forward slowly with the left leg into neko Ashi Dachi.

27 Step forward quickly with the right leg into Migi Zenkutsu Dachi, executing a fast left hand Chudan Nukite, immediately followed by a Migi Chudan Yonhon Nukite, fast.

28 Begin to pivot 180 degrees bringing Migi Yonhon Nukite (spearhand) on top of left back hand.

29 Complete pivot of 180 degrees into Hidari Neko Ashi Dachi, bringing hands down in front of the body and then pull to the right. Slowly and deliberately.

29a Now facing the front again (Shomen).

30 Step forward with right leg into Zenkutsu Dachi and perform right outside block, Soto Uke Chudan, fast.

31 Punch Hidari Gyakuzuki Chudan, fast.

32 Step forward with left leg and execute Hidari Soto Uke Chudan, fast.

33 Punch Migi Gyakuzuki Chudan, fast.

34 Step forward with the right leg into Shiko Dachi stance, looking directly in front and execute Shuto Uke with the right hand, bringing left hand across stomach, fast.

34a Side View.

35 Bring right leg to the right and strike Washide with the right hand to the throat (eagle beak), pulling left fist back on to hip, fast.

36 Keep hands in position and execute Hidari Maegeri Chudan, fast. Kiai.

37 Bring kicking leg back into Zenkutsu Dachi and execute Hidari Gyakuzuki Chudan, fast.

38 Pull left leg across behind, pivoting body 90 degrees into Shiko Dachi and execute a Hazushi-Uke (breaking block), fast.

38a Side View.

39 Step with the right leg diagonally across the left and prepare to execute Shuto Uke.

40 Block Shuto Uke fast in Migi Neko Ashi Dachi. As in U24.

41 Pull back right leg into Heisoku Dachi and execute Hidari Chudan Yonhon Nukite, fast. As in U25.

42 (Step forward slowly with the left leg into Neko Ashi Dachi). As in U26. (Shown from reverse)

43 Step forward quickly with the right leg into Migi Zenkutsu Dachi, executing a fast Hidari Chudan Nukite, immediately followed by a Migi Chudan Yonhon Nukite, fast. As in U27.

44 Bring left leg across, preparing to turn 180 degrees.

44a Rear View.

45 Step down into Shiko Dachi and execute Hidari Haito Uke Chudan, bringing Migi Shuto across stomach, fast.

45a Rear View.

46 Step across with the right leg, slowly, keeping hands in position and not raising height.

47 Transfer all weight on to right leg and block Shuto Uke Jodan, pulling right fist on to hip, do not raise height.

48 Step down with the left leg into Shiko Dachi and execute Migi Yonhon Nukite Chudan, placing left fist on hip, back of the fist facing forwards, fast.

49 Block Migi Haito Uke Chudan, bringing Hidari Shuto across stomach, fast.

50 Step across with the left leg slowly and deliberately, do not move arms or raise height.

51 Transfer all weight on to left leg, blocking Hidari Shuto Uke Jodan, bringing right fist on to hip, do not raise height.

52 Step down with the right leg into Shiko Dachi and execute Migi Chudan Yonhon Nukite, bringing left fist on to hip, back of the fist facing forwards, fast.

53 Slide right leg forward, preparing to block, as at the beginning, slowly and deliberately.

54 Step into Migi Zenkutsu Dachi and execute Uraken Jodan, slowly and deliberately.

55 Pull right leg directly behind, bringing left arm across body.

56 Step into Shiko Dachi looking directly in front and strike left hammer fist (Hidari Tettsui Chudan), fast.

57 Step forward with right leg directly in front into Shiko Dachi and execute Migi Tettsui Uchi Chudan

58 Remaining in Shiko Dachi, slide backwards, executing Hazushi-Uke (breaking block), fast.

58a Side View.

59 Move left leg across, twisting into Hidari Gyakuzuki Dachi and execute right rising Jodan Empi.

59a Reverse View.

60 Pull left leg back into Hidari Neko Ashi and bring both hands up to shoulder height, fully extended and pull back on to hip (all one movement) and executed slowly.

60a Reverse View.

61 Step forward with right leg into Migi Zenkutsu Dachi and execute double spearhand strike (Yonhon Nukite Chudan), fast and Kiai.

61a Reverse View.

62 Pivot 180 degrees into Hidari Neko Ashi Dachi, bringing hands down in front of the body and then pull to the right. Slowly and deliberately (facing front).

63 Pull left leg back into Heisoku Dachi, pressing right fist into open left hand (Yame).

Kata Notes

PASSAI (BASSAI DAI)

Another Kata whose origins are believed to be Tomari. The originator is unknown, but the Kata is widely practised by all Shuri karate schools. Its Japanese name, Bassai (to storm a fortress) is very apt, as the techniques are both powerful and fast.

Characteristics are rapid stance changes with fast block and counter combinations. A trait of Tomari is shown by the Yama Tsuki techniques towards the end of the Kata.

WANSHU (EMPI)

This kata is named after the Chinese military attaché posted in Okinawa in the 18th Century. It is practised in the Tomari region of Okinawa.

Its characteristics are the Gedan Tsuki dropping low and the Jodan Tsuki. Unfortunately, the Maegeris which were once common to Wanshu (regardless of which style practised it) have now been dropped by many schools, replaced by a fast step. I have kept the Maegeri in the Kata shown. The Kata again has nice rhythm changes with powerful combinations of strikes, kicks and punches.

JI'IN

The history of this kata is believed to be linked to those of the kata Jion and Jitte and originates from China.

Ji'in is part of the advanced kata curriculum for Washinkai students. Although an advanced kata, the actual techniques themselves are not difficult to execute. However, the mastery of rhythm changes in Waza (technique) requires hours of practice.

The characteristics are spins, followed by either strikes or blocks, open-handed blocks and rapid stance changes. There are continuous powerful combinations requiring both speed and strength. The kata is active in Shito Ryu, Shukokai and Shotokan schools.

Many Wado schools are now adopting Ji'in as the fast hip and hand movements make it quite natural for the style.

ROHAI (MEIKYO)

Unfortunately, not much is known about the history of Rohai, except that it has been taught in Okinawa since the 18th Century. It is practised in the Tomari and Shuri area of Okinawa.

Rohai is a comparatively short kata in the Shorin Ryu system. The characteristics are Haito Uke (ridge hand blocks) and Sagi Ashi (crane stance), as well as Yama-tsuki (double punches). Like Wanshu, another Tomari Kata, there was a Tobi Shuto Uke {now replaced by the Mikazuki Geri (crescent kick)} and a step at the end of this Kata. Rohai is practised by the majority of the Shuri school of karate. Naha groups do not use it. Fast rhythm changes make this a lovely Kata to both watch and execute. Although one of the shorter kata, great skill is required, as the Kata builds up to two powerful Shuto Uke.

USEISHI (GOJU-SHI-HO)

The Tomari Kata Useishi (Gojushiho) is one of the most advanced Kata of any system. The title means '54', but it is not known whether this is the amount of movements in the Kata or the number given to this Kata in a system that once existed or the 54 vital point strikes hidden in the Kata. It is not used by many schools as far as I know, except for Shito Ryu and Shotokan, which have two versions: Gojushiho-Sho and Gojushiho-Dai.

Again, the origins of the Kata are unknown, except that it is very old and the Chinese influence is quite apparent.

Its characteristics are Yonhon Nukite techniques and the use of Washide (eagle hand strike). It has big, slow, graceful movements as well as fast powerful blocks and strikes. The combinations are both explosive and fast. With such a varied style encompassed within Useishi, it is extremely lovely to perform and aesthetic to watch.

JI-YU KUMITE (Free Fighting)

In my opinion, Ji-Yu Kumite is an essential part of karate training and also a karate-ka's development. Emphasis must be placed upon Ji-Yu Kumite at all levels of a student's progress, starting with simple techniques and building up degrees of difficulty. Initially, the fear of fighting, regardless of how tame, has to be overcome, which is a major obstacle for some students. This is why I stated at the beginning of the book that equal training time must be given to all three subjects, Renraku Waza, Yakusoku Kumite and Kata.

Kumite, although considered dangerous by some, can be most enjoyable to practise. Pitting your wits against an opponent is invigorating and challenging.

Karate is a Martial Art and certain techniques are far too dangerous to use in Ji-Yu Kumite practice and therefore prohibited.

Nevertheless, there are many techniques (Waza) that can be used whilst practising your Ji-Yu Kumite.

Besides your basic skills such as kicks (Keri) and punches (Tsuki) there are strikes (Uchi), hip-shift (Taisabaki), (flowing) bodyshifting (Nagashi), (escaping) (Nogare), entering (Irimi) and evasion (Kawashi), techniques to be practised. Practising Ji-Yu Kumite at other clubs and with other styles is also beneficial.

Obviously, your skills will improve with regular practice and as you climb the grading ladder. The main ingredients for successful application in Ji-Yu Kumite are the same as in Yakusoku Kumite – speed, timing, distance, accuracy and confidence. However, over-confidence can work against you.

When your confidence builds, it is quite easy to become totally immersed in Ji-Yu Kumite practice and what seems like a five minute sparring session often turns out to be an hour.

To be proficient in Ji-Yu Kumite alone, in my opinion, does not make you a true karate-ka. A rounded karate-ka practises both kata and kumite and it usually shows in his demeanour.

SUMMARY

It is a sad fact that many karate instructors, regardless of style, are very insular about their training methods. The slogan 'this is the only true style or way' is still heard regularly.

The Shu Ha Ri maxim only applies to certain instructors when it suits. Unfortunately, preaching it is one thing, accepting its concept when students follow the Shu Ha Ri path is another.

Karate knowledge is infinitesimal and the serious student strives to achieve as much knowledge as possible in a lifetime. However, if a student is terrified of branching out to see other schools' methods of karate training because it would displease 'Sensei', then his knowledge must be restricted.

On the other hand, students who attend the dojo from other styles should not be shunned if they show they are serious and intend to train regularly.

I have no qualms about passing knowledge to serious students and there are many senior karate-ka in the UK who, though from a different ryu (school) have incorporated many of my ideas and techniques into their systems. To me this is not boasting, but following the true ideals of karate-do. I am simply treating others in the same way I was treated once I left the severe restraints of a particular 'way'.

This approach strengthens groups and associations, not weakens them. Groups still retain their own identity and their students feel more accomplished having spread their wings, yet there is extreme loyalty to both association and instructor, as they are being treated as individuals. Each association has something different to offer and quite often can explain certain aspects of karate in a different way, making either the technique or the philosophy much easier to understand. This must be taken advantage of and I fully encourage students to train with reputable instructors of different schools.

To become a good and proficient student of karate-do requires determination, self-discipline and, usually, a lot of sacrifice. Yet this is a small price to pay for producing a 'whole person', skilled in the physical aspects of karate and retaining a high moral standard.

Author at the London Judokan 1972

*Author with Seiji Sugimoto at the Shotokan Karate International Headquarters,
Yotsuya Dojo, Tokyo 1988.*

Author with Teruo Hayashi, 10th Dan, Headmaster of Hayashi-Ha Shitoryu, London 1994.

Author demonstrating Tameshiwari (wood breaking) at Washinkai National Championship 1997.